W9-AAR-642

NOT YOUR Mama's KITCHEN

THE ESSENTIAL GUIDE TO GET YOURS STARTED

LYNN DUGAN

REGISTERED DIETITIAN/CHEF

All rights reserved. This book or any portion thereof may not be reproduced or used in any manner whatsoever without the express written permission of the publisher except for the use of brief quotations in a book review.

ISBN: 978-1-54398--612-9

Acknowledgements

This book would not have been possible without the help I have received from my family and friends. My husband, Jack, and four kids—Becca, Courtney, John and Matthew—gave me the foundation and inspiration I needed to complete this project: they listened to my ideas, tasted my recipes, and often patiently waited for me to take photos of our dinner before anyone could eat. Becca was also my copy editor. Thank you! I am forever grateful!

Thanks to Mom & Dad, my sisters & brother, and their families for their support and encouragement.

Thank you, Elle Friedel, my editor who boldly gave me a calendar in which to work and keep me on track.

Thank you to the nutrition students (who are now RDN's or very close) who have helped me with recipe development and videography: Hailey Gorski, Emily Mattaliano, Emma McCarthy, Frankie Severyns and Kayla Turrell.

Thank you to my friends at Marcel's Culinary Experience for the opportunity to share my love of food and nutrition with the Marcel's community.

Thank you to the Nutrition Department at Benedictine University for the privilege of teaching undergraduates who have given me a first-hand understanding of their challenges and strengths in the kitchen.

Thank you to these friends who provided early manuscript and recipe feedback: Meredith Maltby, Beth Phillips, and Rachel Thompson.

And thank you to my colleagues who have cheered me on at key moments in this journey: Chere Bork, Robin Brown, Anne Cundiff, Stephanie Cundith, Jane Gooder, Jen Haugen, Betsy Hornick, Cathy Leman, Jacqueline Marcus, Jodie Sheild, Linda Van Horn, and the Glenbard District 87 Wellness Committee.

Thanks to God for all these people and for His ultimate guidance in writing this book!

TABLE OF CONTENTS

INTRODUCTION

Did your mom cook delicious food for you growing up or did she not cook at all? Were homemade dinners provided every night or was the pizza delivery number on speed dial? Chances are it was somewhere in the middle. Whatever you grew up with, your own kitchen is different.

These days, you have recipes at your fingertips on your smartphone or tablet. You may have learned to cook from short videos on social media. Your palate is more international, adventurous and discerning. You like good food, but with a busy schedule, you don't have all day to spend in the kitchen. You want real food: food that's not only tasty but also interesting and unique.

You live in an incredibly digital age and are driven to the kitchen more than ever. The kitchen is your social center. It grounds you. When friends gather to cook and eat together, food becomes more than just sustenance and routine. You need recipes that entice and delight, but you also hope to spend wisely and stretch your dollar when buying ingredients. Because you care about health, you want to separate the nutrition facts from fads. Because you care about the environment, you think twice about food packaging and kitchen waste.

You likely have fond memories of the childhood food your parents made, such as your birthday cake, Sunday family dinners, or holiday treats. Those foods will never be replaced or forgotten. However, for your everyday meals, you need recipes and food inspiration that work in your own kitchen.

That is why *Not Your Mama's Kitchen* is here for you. You'll learn to make tasty food that is nutritious, time-saving, environmentally-friendly, and budget-conscious. You'll also discover new foods and ways to prepare and enjoy them. Turn the page and let's get started!

CHAPTER 1

Nutrition:

GET THE FACTS

I decided to pursue a career in nutrition when I was a sophomore in high school. My dad had recently been diagnosed with high cholesterol, significantly changing our family's diet. We regularly ate balanced meals but began to substitute chicken and fish for our usual sausage, steak, and hamburgers. My mom's amazing homemade desserts (cakes, pies, ice cream and cookies) were replaced with fresh fruit. Intrigued by how food could treat a medical diagnosis, I pursued the study of nutrition. I became a Registered Dietitian/Nutritionist after completing my post-graduate internship and passing a national exam. Because nutrition is a science, the field continues to expand. As science progresses, the role of the Registered Dietitian is to translate that science to practical application, making healthy eating a reality for others. This is my mission.

The topic of nutrition receives a lot of chatter, which does not always come from the experts. There is noise everywhere on how to eat, what to eat, and what foods to avoid. This results in fear, confusion, and misguided eating habits. We have lost focus on simple eating: whole foods prepared with fresh ingredients. That should be our focus.

A Place to Begin

The US Dietary Guidelines[1] provides us with an outline for what a nutritious diet looks like. These guidelines are revised every five years, so be sure to check the most recent version. It defines healthy eating as consuming foods from each of the following food groups:

- **Vegetables:** *include a variety of colors, legumes and starchy vegetables*
    - *Colors: dark green (spinach & kale), red (beets & tomatoes) and orange (sweet potatoes & carrots)*
    - *Legumes: beans & soy, lentils & chick peas*
    - *Starchy Vegetables: corn & potatoes*

- **Fruits**: *whole fruits are preferred over fruit juice*
- **Grains**: *at least half should be whole grains; including brown rice, whole wheat, oats, barley, and quinoa*
- **Dairy**: *low-fat or fat-free: milk, yogurt, cheese and/or fortified soy beverages*
- **Protein**: *include different sources, such as seafood, lean meats and poultry, eggs, legumes (from the vegetable category, also rich in protein), nuts and seeds*
- **Oils**: *from plants; including olive, canola, soybean and sunflower*

Follow MyPlate

USDA MyPlate

The United States Department of Agriculture (USDA) has developed MyPlate to show us what healthy eating looks like. Half of our plate should be filled with fruits and vegetables, the other half divided between protein and grains. Of the grains we eat, at least 50% should be whole grains.[1] Whole grains refer to grains with their outer bran layer intact. In contrast, refined grains have the bran layer removed, such as in white rice or white flour. The dairy section on the plate reminds us to consume 3 servings of dairy each day.

MyPlate eating focuses on consuming foods that are nutrient dense. These are foods that are close to their natural state. They have rich nutrient contents that have not been processed or prepared with extra solid fats, added sugars, refined grains and salt.[1]

Many foods we eat aren't on MyPlate. Even though foods such as coffee, cookies, chips, sports drinks, ice cream, soda or wine don't fit into any of the food groups on the plate, they are not "bad" foods. In fact, there are no "bad" foods in our diet. However, there are bad diets. A bad diet is when foods not included in MyPlate regularly replace foods that should be on the plate, for example, eating chips instead of an apple.

MyPlate illustrates the ideal quality of our eating. When wondering how much food to eat per day, consider how many calories you should consume. Calories are a measure of the energy we get from the macronutrients in food. Fats provide 9 calories per gram, more than twice the amount provided by carbohydrates and protein (4 calories per gram). The daily number of calories you need is individualized and based on height, weight, age, gender and activity level. That amount accounts for the calories you expend during activity, in addition to your basal metabolic rate: the quantity of energy your body requires at rest. Below, I provide a summary for someone requiring 2,000 calories a day (the amount of calories needed for a moderately-active adult weighing about 130 pounds). This is also the number of calories used by the US Food and Drug Administration (FDA) as their standard for the information seen on food labels.

> **Vegetables: 2 ½ cups** (1 cup = 1 cup raw, cooked or canned vegetables OR 2 cups salad greens OR 1 cup 100% vegetable juice)

> **Fruit: 2 cups** (1 cup = 1 cup raw, frozen, cooked or canned fruit OR ½ cup dried fruit OR 1 cup 100% fruit juice)

> **Grains: 6 ounces** (1 ounce = 1 slice of bread OR 1 ounce ready-to-eat cereal OR ½ cup cooked rice, pasta or cereal)

> **Dairy: 3 cups** (1 cup = 1 cup milk OR 1 cup yogurt OR 1 cup fortified soy beverage OR 1 ½ ounces natural cheese)

> **Protein: 5 ½ ounces** (1 ounce = 1 ounce cooked or canned lean meat, poultry or seafood OR 1 egg OR 1 tablespoon nut butter OR ¼ cup cooked beans or peas OR ½ ounce nuts or seeds)

A great online resource to calculate your individual calorie needs is the MyPlate Plan, that can be accessed on the USDA MyPlate website.[2] It will also provide an adjusted breakdown by MyPlate food groups, as done above with the 2,000-calorie example, according to your individual recommended daily calories.

Know What You Eat: Nutrition Facts Label

Nutrition Facts

8 servings per container
Serving size   2/3 cup (55g)

Amount per serving
Calories   **230**

% Daily Value*

Total Fat 8g	**10%**
Saturated Fat 1g	**5%**
Trans Fat 0g	
Cholesterol 0mg	**0%**
Sodium 160mg	**7%**
Total Carbohydrate 37g	**13%**
Dietary Fiber 4g	**14%**
Total Sugars 12g	
Includes 10g Added Sugars	**20%**
Protein 3g	
Vitamin D 2mcg	10%
Calcium 260mg	20%
Iron 8mg	45%
Potassium 240mg	6%

* The % Daily Value (DV) tells you how much a nutrient in a serving of food contributes to a daily diet. 2,000 calories a day is used for general nutrition advice.

In addition to MyPlate, another great resource for healthy eating is the Nutrition Facts food label, which is produced by the FDA on all packaged foods. The food label is a valuable tool to empower you while making food choices in the grocery store. Choose foods that are higher in fiber, vitamins and minerals and that are lower in saturated fat, added sugar and sodium. To understand what you are eating, consider that the ingredients list is ordered by weight, from those present in the largest to smallest amounts.

Nutrition Facts label

Nutrients on the label are quantified in amounts per serving as well as the percent Daily Value (DV). The Daily Value tells us how much a nutrient in a serving of that food contributes to our daily needs. Refer to the Nutrition Facts label pictured here. On this label, one serving contains 4 grams of dietary fiber, providing 14% DV. The Daily Value for dietary fiber is 25 grams. When selecting whole grain foods, such as breakfast cereals, look for at least 3 grams of fiber per serving. In addition, check the amount of added sugar. Added sugar occurs during processing of the food and does not include any natural sugars from fruits or dairy. The recommendation for added sugar is to limit it to 12.5 teaspoons, or 50 grams, daily.

When it comes to processed food, reading food labels is the only way to know what you're eating. Of course, the more fresh, nutrient-dense foods you eat, the less labels you have, which is more desirable for healthy eating. In order to follow these guidelines, make small changes that work for you and that will stick with you over time.

Sorting Out the Facts

What's the truth about dairy? The Guidelines recommend 3 servings of dairy each day for everyone over 9 years of age.[1] Dairy foods help meet calcium, vitamin D and potassium needs—nutrients we generally aren't getting enough of. While many people, with a goal of healthy eating, have cut dairy foods from their diet, the truth is eating low-fat and fat-free dairy is linked with a reduction in chronic diseases such as type 2 diabetes.[3]

Dairy shelves in the grocery store are filled with dairy substitutes that have gained popularity. They are products sold as "milk", and they are made from plants (like almond, oat, coconut and cashew). Key nutrients which are found in milk may be missing in dairy substitutes. Calcium is found naturally in cow's milk dairy, and plant-based beverages need to be fortified with calcium. Look for 300mg calcium per serving or about 30% DV on dairy substitutes. Vitamin D is not always found in plant-based beverages, but it is fortified in natural dairy foods in varying amounts: typically 100 IU or 30% DV.[4]

While you may think a milk made from nuts such as almonds or cashews would be high in protein, it is actually significantly less. The protein content of milk and soy milk is 8 grams per serving, while both almond and cashew milk has 1 gram of protein per serving. If you have a dairy allergy or intolerance and need to consume a plant-based dairy substitute, it is always wise to check the Nutrition Facts label to be sure you are still consuming the nutrients you need.

What about people who are lactose-intolerant? Fermented dairy foods such as yogurt and kefir—a fermented milk drink resembling a thin yogurt—contain probiotics, which are active bacteria cultures. These living microorganisms can digest lactose (natural milk sugar), which allows some people who are lactose-intolerant to enjoy these dairy foods.[5]

Some common diets also prohibit gluten, grains and legumes. Unless there is an allergy or intolerance, no clinical evidence indicates that avoiding these foods is healthier. In fact, legumes and whole grains, even those containing gluten, have been consistently linked to positive health outcomes.

Can a vegetarian diet meet all needs? With careful planning, the answer is yes! There are some nutrients you must be intentional about consuming in your diet, especially if you're a strict vegan. A diet void of animal products will eliminate the most available form of iron.[6] Plant forms of iron are dried beans, peas, lentils, enriched cereals, dark green leafy vegetables and dried fruit. As already discussed, the calcium and vitamin D from dairy foods need to be found in well-fortified dairy substitutes. When you use salt in cooking, use iodized salt to get needed iodine. Also, no plant foods are a secure form of vitamin B12 naturally found in salmon, trout, beef, eggs and dairy foods. You will need to consume fortified foods or supplements for adequate B12 to avoid a deficiency.[7] A Registered Dietitian/Nutritionist can help you with a well-guided meal plan to meet all your nutrient needs.

When at the grocery store, you may be wondering whether or not the higher price of organic foods is worth it for health benefits. In general, it is always better to consume fruits and vegetables than to avoid them. So, if you don't want to pay extra for organic foods, then eat conventional produce. When I go grocery shopping, I focus on buying organic primarily for the fruits and vegetables that are included on the "dirty dozen" list published and updated annually by the Environmental Working Group.[8] The organic produce I buy is from the top of that list and typically includes strawberries, spinach, apples and grapes.

Let's look at what the dietary guidelines suggest we should limit in our eating. We are advised to keep saturated fat intake in check and cut down on added sugar and sodium.[1]

Saturated fat is found mostly in animal protein foods, including red meat, poultry with skin, cream and butter. Saturated fats are solid at room temperature, like what you see when the grease from bacon cools. Tropical oils, such as coconut and palm oil, also contain saturated fat.[9] You can limit saturated fat by purchasing lean cuts of meat and varying protein choices to include legumes and fish. Choosing to cook with a liquid vegetable oil, such as olive, soybean, or canola (containing monounsaturated and/or polyunsaturated fats) instead of regularly using butter and coconut oil is another smart way to decrease your consumption of saturated fat. When following MyPlate, saturated fat is naturally limited by eating a plate filled with plant foods.

The recommendation to cut down on sugar includes any added sugar, as described above, but it does not include cutting down on natural sugars found in foods such as fruit and dairy. With a recommendation of only 12.5 teaspoons daily, this can add up quickly if you enjoy sweet desserts and sugary beverages. Hidden sugars count as well, such as those found in jarred pasta sauces, energy drinks, canned fruit in syrup, and breakfast cereals.

In regard to sodium, the recommendation for maximum sodium consumption is 2,300mg daily, which is the amount found in one teaspoon of salt. While it helps to avoid the saltshaker at the table, most of the sodium in American diets comes from processed and packaged foods. These include frozen meals, canned or pickled foods, condiments and snacks. Reducing the amount of sodium in your diet may initially cause foods to taste bland, but over time, your taste will adapt, and you'll be able to use less salt for the same flavor. When cooking pasta, avoid adding salt to the water. Rinsing canned beans before using significantly reduces their sodium content. It will also be important to rely on herbs and other seasonings to bring more flavor to your palette with less salt, just as what's done with the recipes in this book, like the *Black Bean Cakes with Spicy Yogurt Sauce* (page 56). Even when salt is included in any of my recipes, it is often added at the very end of cooking "to taste". There are so many ways to enhance flavors of dishes beyond salt, and you will discover these in many recipes on my website, www.myplate2yours.com. One of my favorites is *Ancho Pork and Hominy Stew*, which can be found at the back of this book (page 88).

No Fancy Diet or Meal Plan Needed

All foods can fit into a healthy diet. It's about balance and plant-based eating. Focus on nutrient-dense fruits, vegetables, whole grains, and good sources of protein, including plant foods (legumes, nuts and seeds), lean meats, poultry and fish. Three daily servings of dairy foods (or a calcium-rich substitute) are also important. While you should purchase as few foods with labels as possible, be smart when reading the labels and comparing them to other foods to know what you are consuming. Reduce the amount of saturated fat, added sugar, and sodium in your diet. With these principles in mind, you will be set up for success.

When the next popular diet catches your attention, compare it to these recommendations. If one of the food groups found on MyPlate is eliminated, approach the diet with caution. If you have specific nutrition concerns, seek the help of a Registered Dietitian/Nutritionist.

Eating in this way can keep you energized and healthy in the short-term to help you succeed in what you do, but it can have long-term benefits as well. Many chronic health problems including heart disease, cancer, diabetes, obesity, and osteoporosis can be prevented with this healthy diet. Just focus on the food groups you should be getting each day from MyPlate. It's that simple: no fancy diet or meal plan. Enjoy!

CHAPTER 2

Welcome to the Kitchen:

ESSENTIAL EQUIPMENT AND UTENSILS

The first recipe I remember trying to make was a birthday cake when I was thirteen years old. My best friend and I wanted to make a cake from scratch for one of our friends. It was a disaster! We used a baking pan that was too large. The result was a cookie-thin, hard, brown, baked layer stuck to waxed paper. It was totally inedible but a valuable learning experience. We quickly realized that the use of proper kitchen equipment is necessary for success. This lesson has helped me throughout my career, and I'm sure it has for her as well, as she also became a Registered Dietitian/Nutritionist.

Welcome to the kitchen: it's time to start! Let's take a look at essential equipment and handy utensils you will need.

Knives

The first piece of equipment you need is a good chef knife. Don't be afraid of this essential kitchen tool. A chef knife can be used for cutting, slicing, chopping, mincing and dicing. Most people are comfortable with a 6- or 8-inch knife, but some use a 10-inch knife. Traditionally, a good knife is made of carbon steel or stainless steel. Ceramic knives also have gained popularity. They are significantly lighter in weight and tend to stay sharp longer. However, they are less durable as they can break if dropped or can become notched from hitting a bone in meat or the pit of a fruit while cutting. When purchasing a ceramic knife, choose carefully, as some knives marketed as ceramic are made of stainless steel and have a ceramic nonstick coating. These don't keep their sharp edge like a true ceramic blade.

A new knife is sharp when purchased, but you'll need a plan for sharpening their blades once they become dull with repeated use. You can find knife-sharpening services in shoe repair shops or other retail outlets. You can also purchase tools to sharpen your own knives at home. A sharp knife is safer than a dull one due to its precision. When sharp, it promotes proper cutting techniques, requiring the right amount of force with a slicing (not sawing) motion. Dull knives are more likely to slip, which increases the chance of injury.

Besides a chef knife, two other knives are nice to have: a paring knife and a serrated knife. A paring knife is used for jobs such as mincing garlic and other small veggies or prepping herbs. A serrated knife is useful for slicing bread, bagels, cake, or cheese. These two knives are optional, because your chef knife can effectively do all of that too.

You can spend from $10 to over $100 on good knives. Start within your budget. Chefs have their favorite knives, but you don't need to be as particular in your kitchen.

Cutting Boards

A good cutting board is the necessary partner for your new knife. There are many choices: wood, bamboo, plastic or glass.

Wood is an overall good choice for your first board. It is always appropriate for cutting bread, produce and cheese. Wood is more porous than plastic, so it may be more likely to harbor bacteria if not washed properly after cutting raw meats, chicken and fish. Maple, teak and acacia are considered harder and better woods.[10] You can place wooden boards in the dishwasher, but you run the risk of the boards drying and cracking over time.

Bamboo has become a more affordable and eco-friendly option for cutting boards. It's harder than most wood but not dishwasher-safe.

Plastic is another inexpensive option. I prefer plastic boards for cutting raw meats because they are easy to clean. They're not porous and can be put into the dishwasher for extra sanitation. The downside to plastic cutting boards is that they're easily damaged and will need to be replaced. Your knife will create grooves in the board over time.

Glass is not recommended for cutting boards. It's extremely hard and likely to damage your knife.

Pots & Pans

Pans: Start with a 10-inch, non-stick skillet. This pan can be used for anything from scrambling eggs to sautéing vegetables. Teflon is a common material for non-stick pans. Health concerns over PFOA (a material historically found in Teflon) led to the popularity of ceramic-coated pans, which are a more expensive option. Not to worry, since 2013, all Teflon products on the market are made PFOA-free.[11] Non-stick pans can be used safely on the cooktop. To protect any non-stick pan, don't use metal utensils while cooking, as they can scratch the surface. For clean-up, don't wash the pan in the dishwasher. Instead, clean it with a soft, non-abrasive cloth and dishwashing liquid.

Pots: A traditional 3- to 4-quart saucepan with tall sides will serve you well in the kitchen for soup, chili, pasta, rice, and much more! Don't forget to choose a pot that includes a lid. The best saucepans have bottoms that are as thick as the sides, which ensures even heat distribution.

Measuring Cups

Dry Measuring Cups: These are used to measure any ingredients that are not liquid. Dry measuring cups are typically sold as a set with 1, ½, 1/3 and ¼ cup measures. When making the recipes in this book, you can use the dry measuring cups to measure rice, shredded cheese, egg noodles and baby spinach. Best practice is to completely fill the cup to the top for accuracy without overflowing the cup. Two dry ingredients that require different methods are brown sugar and flour. For brown sugar, use a spoon to push down and pack it in the cup until it reaches the top. Conversely, for flour, gently spoon it into the cup (without packing it), and then use a knife or the straight handle of the spoon to level it off.

Liquid Measuring Cups: These are typically found as incremented 1-cup or 2-cup volumes with a handle and pouring spout. When filling the cup with liquid, make sure the cup is secure on a flat surface, and not just being held in your hand. Liquids tend to slightly dip, or bow, when in a cup. The lowest point of the bow (called the meniscus) is the correct measure. Position the cup at eye level to assess this measurement. These are typically made of Pyrex or plastic. Pyrex is a tempered glass that withstands heat.

Tableware and Flatware

This is an important category, because how would you eat the meal you just prepared without dishes and forks, knives, or spoons? Once you cook your meal, you need equipment to eat it with! Melamine is a low-cost plastic commonly used to make plates. While it is a less-expensive and durable option, it is not microwave-safe or eco-friendly (it can't be recycled and isn't found naturally in our environment). Better options are bamboo or ceramic plates, which are more environmentally-conscious. For flatware (including forks, knives and spoons), choose any type within your budget.

A restaurant supply store is a good place to find better-quality, cost-conscious flatware. If you live alone, purchase at least 4 sets of flatware and tableware (4 of each item in the list below). If you live with one other person, purchase at least 6-8 sets of flatware and tableware. Make sure your bowls are big enough for cereal and soup.

The List

The recommendations in this list prepare you, not just for the recipes in this book, but for all your essential cooking needs. While you can look in places such as Target or Amazon for the knives, pots and pans, many of the other items listed below can be purchased inexpensively at a dollar store and be perfectly effective in your kitchen.

- *Chef Knife: 6- or 8-inch*
- *Paring Knife (optional)*
- *Serrated Knife (optional)*
- *Cutting Boards (hard wood, bamboo, or plastic)*

- *Mixing Bowls: small, medium, and large (often sold as a nesting set ranging from about 6 to 12 inches in diameter)*

- *Dry Measuring Cups Set (metal or plastic)*
- *Liquid Measuring Cup (Pyrex or plastic)*
- *Measuring Spoons Set (metal or plastic)*

- *Skillet: 10-inch, non-stick (Teflon or ceramic-coated)*
- *Saucepan with Lid: 3 to 4 quarts*

- *Baking Sheet (preferably the rimmed version, which is multi-use, compared to flat sheets which are specifically for baking)*
- *Baking Pan: 9-inch x 13-inch (Pyrex)*

- *Instant-Read Thermometer (an easy-to-read digital tool and a must-have for food safety and quality)*

- *Spatula/Pancake Turner**
- *Large Cooking Spoon**
- *Large Slotted Cooking Spoon**
- *Tongs**
- *Vegetable Peeler*

- Can Opener

Choose wooden, nylon, silicone or coated utensils to preserve the non-stick skillet

- Medium Colander (useful for rinsing beans/produce and draining pasta/lentils after cooking)
- Small Jar with Lid (reuse a salsa jar for no additional cost)
- Parchment Paper and Aluminum Foil
- Paper Towels
- Kitchen Towels
- Oven Mitts and Pot Holders

- Dinner Plates
- Lunch/Salad Plates (great to use for smaller/lighter meals)
- Cereal/Soup Bowls
- Forks, Knives, Spoons

Extras: the items on this list are not essential but can be used often in your kitchen.

- Box Grater (useful for grating cheese/ginger and for zesting citrus)
- Kitchen Shears (heavy scissors used for anything from dividing a chicken thigh to clipping herbs)
- Pastry Brush (useful for brushing oil on garlic bread or barbecue sauce on chicken)
- Food Storage Containers
- Hand Mixer
- Stand Blender
- Toaster
- Skewers

You've made it through the list! I've got a treat for you. In the back of this book is a *Chocolate Lava Cake* (page 90) recipe that I've created, which is much improved from my first failed attempt many years ago.

CHAPTER 3

How To:

PREPPING AND COOKING TECHNIQUES

In 2012, I interviewed for my first chef position as an instructor at a cooking school. I had 30 minutes to create something that reflected my culinary style and flavor. The response I got from the executive chef after she tasted my dish (Tofu and Cashew Lettuce Cups, page 91) was, "I love your style, I really like your food, but your knife skills are atrocious!" I was stumped, did I get the job or not? She asked me to come back to the kitchen the next day with a variety of produce. In the morning, I showed up with peppers, melons, onions, herbs and potatoes. We spent a few hours dicing, chopping, and mincing. It was a necessary crash course in knife skills as I began a new job teaching cooking classes!

Knife skills will revolutionize your kitchen experience. Start by holding your chef knife with your fingers around the handle; your index finger and thumb should grip the base of the blade. Stand squarely in front of the counter and always cut away from you. Keep your hands dry so the knife doesn't slip. Learning proper knife skills saves time in the kitchen and keeps you safe. This is an essential cooking technique we all need to learn. I have a video to help you with this skill on my website *www.myplate2yours.com*.

As you prepare to cook in your kitchen, consider whether your cooktop/stovetop and oven are gas or electric. Electric cooktops and ovens take longer to heat than gas. They also take longer to adjust to temperature changes on the cooktop, such as going from a boil to a simmer. Sometimes it's best to switch to a different electric burner if cooking temperatures need to change quickly. With either gas or electric, always match your pan size with the correct size burner. Avoid using a burner with a diameter larger than the bottom of the pan.

Cooktops are used for sautéing, stir-frying, simmering (soups, chilis, sauces), and preparing pasta, rice and other grains. Ovens are used for roasting, baking and broiling. Here are the basic cooking skills you will encounter when creating the recipes in this book:

Sauté and Stir-fry

Sauté and stir-fry are similar skills. Both involve using a small amount of oil in a pan over medium-high heat. Food is cooked by moving it around with a spatula or wooden spoon to cook it evenly and control the degree of cooking. It's an easy way to prevent vegetables from overcooking and keep them tender-crisp. The term "stir-fry" is usually used in reference to a wok or deep skillet. A stir-fry traditionally calls for a slightly higher heat than a sauté due to the larger size of the pan.

Simmer and Boil

Simmering is a term to describe cooking soups, stews and liquids just below a boil, often referred to as a "gentle boil". Simmering is also used in the poached chicken recipe as described below. Boiling is the method for cooking pasta and hard-boiled eggs.

How to Poach Chicken Breasts

Poaching chicken makes it tasty and tender. It is a healthy cooking technique, as no extra fat is required when cooking the chicken. Poached chicken breasts are used in *Pasta Salad with Chicken & Veggies* (page 42). They can also be added to *Veggie Pasta Bowl* (page 46) and *Entrée Spinach Salad* (page 48).

To poach, arrange the chicken in a single layer on the bottom of the pot. Add salt and pepper and any aromatics, such as minced garlic, bay leaf, thinly sliced onion, and/or fresh or dried herbs. Add water to cover chicken by 1 inch. Bring water to a boil. Cover and reduce heat to a simmer. Cook for 10-15 minutes, until the temperature of the chicken is 165 degrees Fahrenheit (°F). Remove chicken from the broth and serve warm or store in a sealed container in the fridge.

How to Cook Pasta

Fill a saucepan with hot water. Place pan on the cooktop and heat to boiling. Once the water is boiling, add the desired quantity of pasta and stir. There should be room in the pan for the pasta to move freely in the boiling water. When the water returns to a boil, you may need to slightly reduce the heat to avoid vigorous boiling but to maintain the boil. Check the package directions for cooking time, boxed pasta typically cooks for about 10 minutes. When finished, turn off heat. Place a colander in the sink and drain pasta. Return pasta to pan and it's ready to serve. If you are keeping pasta in the pan for more than 5-10 minutes before serving, mix a drizzle of olive oil into the pasta so it doesn't stick together as it cools.

How to Cook Hard-Boiled Eggs

Hard-boiled eggs can be prepared for the *Entrée Spinach Salad* (page 48), enjoyed for a protein-rich breakfast, or packed unpeeled for a brown bag lunch.

To prepare hard-boiled eggs, place raw eggs* in a saucepan large enough to hold them in single layer. Add cold water to cover eggs by 1 inch. Heat over high heat just until boiling, then remove from burner and cover pan. Let eggs stand in hot water for approximately 9 minutes for medium eggs, 12 minutes for large eggs, or 15 minutes for extra-large eggs. Drain immediately and cool under running water until able to handle. Serve eggs warm or cool completely in cold water, then refrigerate. Unpeeled or peeled cooked eggs can be kept in a sealed container in the refrigerator for up to one week.

Note: refrigerated raw eggs will stay fresh in the refrigerator for about 3 weeks after purchase.

Roasting

Roasting, a technique used in my recipe *Sheet Pan Italian Chicken with Vegetables* (page 71), requires a hot oven and a rimmed baking sheet. Before preheating the oven, place the baking rack in the upper-third portion of the oven. Set the oven temperature to 450°F to preheat. For easy cleanup, line the baking sheet with foil before filling it with any ingredients.

Roasting is a great way to cook a variety of vegetables, including root vegetables (potatoes, carrots, parsnips), green vegetables (asparagus, broccoli, zucchini and brussels sprouts), and more (eggplant, bell peppers and squash). Roasting is also the method used for the sweet potatoes in *Warm Sweet Potato, Lentil and Apple Bowl* (page 60). For these and any other vegetable you want to roast, dice them into a 1-inch size and spread out onto a rimmed baking sheet lined with foil or parchment paper. Vegetables need a roomy, single layer to roast best. To avoid crowding the baking sheet, you may need to divide the veggies into two sheets. Drizzle the veggies with olive oil and add salt and pepper to your liking. Place the sheets high in the oven (preheated to 425°F) and check them after 15 minutes. Be sure to rotate the sheets if using more than one at a time. Cook 10-15 minutes more, as needed. When done, roasted veggies will darken on the edges and be tender when tested with a fork. You may find this to be your favorite way to enjoy vegetables.

Baking

The oven temperature in baking is usually 350-400°F. It is very important to preheat the oven to the proper baking temperature. I have tried to prompt you to do so in the recipes here. During cooking, the baking dish or sheet pan used in the recipe is placed in the center of the oven. Baking is the method used in recipes like *Potato and Egg Bake* (page 43), *Cheddar Chicken & Potato Packets* (page 47), and *Oven Baked Italian Sliders* (page 66).

Broiling

This technique is not needed when making the recipes in the book, but it's easy to use. The broil setting on your oven activates the upper heating elements. Place the sheet pan high in oven, only 3-4 inches from the heat. Do not use parchment paper to line a pan for broiling as it will likely burn. Any food in the broiler should be monitored closely to prevent burning. Thin steaks and open-face toasted cheese are common broiled items. You can even toast bread by using the broiler, but beware, 30 seconds on each side is sufficient.

Steaming

Steaming is a quick method to cook fresh vegetables. They retain their nutrient density because they don't require oil or other fats to cook. Prepare vegetables by cutting them into uniform pieces (broccoli/cauliflower florets, carrot slices, green beans trimmed). Heat 2 cups of water in a saucepan. Bring water to a boil and toss in the veggies of your choice. Immediately put the lid on the pan and allow the veggies to cook for 5 minutes (broccoli, cauliflower and green beans) or 8 minutes (carrots). Lift the lid carefully and test veggies with a fork. When ready, they should be tender with some resistance. Immediately toss veggies into a colander to drain. They are ready to serve!

Mise en Place

When you are finally ready to start preparing a recipe, practice *mise en place*. *Mise en place* (pronounced "meezon plas") is a culinary phrase taken from a French term meaning "everything in its place". This concept models a helpful way to organize every cooking experience. Here's how it can be done.

First, review the recipe. Pull out all necessary equipment and ingredients. Next, get the ingredients ready to be used in the recipe. This may include measuring some ingredients and using your knife to dice or slice others. Finally, you are ready to begin preparing the recipe. *Mise en place* reduces steps in the kitchen and interruptions in the recipe as the ingredients are prepared prior to cooking. This improves efficiency and decreases prep time, allowing you to spend more time enjoying the meal.

CHAPTER 4

Food Safety:

DO NO HARM

Once I lost power for three days in a summer storm. The meats in the freezer thawed and foods in the refrigerator warmed. It was a food safety crisis like I've never seen before! For dinner, I scrambled to use what we had before it warmed completely and went to waste. We ate Arugula Salad with Roasted Beets and Goat Cheese (page 92) using ingredients salvaged from the fridge. It was a dinner I will never forget!

There are daily steps you can take in the kitchen to keep you, your food, and those who consume it safe. I teach an undergraduate nutrition course in a food laboratory and kitchen. We spend the first day in lab reviewing safety and sanitation rules, and everyone has to pass a quiz on food safety to participate in the remainder of the class. I don't have a quiz for you at the end of this chapter, but please read this information carefully. There are three primary areas of kitchen and food safety to know: food preparation, cooking temperatures, and food storage.

Food Preparation

While it takes knowledge and practice to make healthy and delicious meals in your kitchen, the techniques you use to prepare this food are critical to avoiding food-borne illness and contamination. You will need to follow these methods in order to keep you safe in the kitchen and keep your food free from bacteria, so that all who eat it can enjoy it safely!

First and foremost, you, as the chef, need to avoid injuries to yourself while cooking. Don't leave used knives in sinks or any place where they aren't easily seen. Keep long hair pulled back and away from food. Open flames from gas burners also pose a safety risk, especially for small children, pets, or anyone with flowing sleeves, neckties or long hair. Since electric cooktops remain hot for a while after cooking, they may pose a safety hazard if you aren't careful. The bottom line is it's important to be careful with any cooktop.

Now that you are safe from cuts and fire hazards while cooking, let's focus on how to keep the food you make safe for all who consume it. Always start food preparation with clean hands and fingernails: wash your hands for 20 seconds under warm water with an ample amount of soap. Wash hands again every time you cough, sneeze or touch anything that can be a source of food contamination, such as your cell phone.

Wash all produce with cold water, including fresh herbs, greens and sprouts. Make a habit of washing off the tops of cans before opening them, including drink cans.

The safest methods to thaw frozen foods are in the refrigerator, microwave, or with cold water. If using a microwave to thaw frozen food, there is often a defrost setting to use. This is a quick method to thaw frozen protein. It's important to note that the microwave will make the outer portion of the protein hot, so it will need to be cooked immediately after thawing. Another thawing method is the use of cold water. You can thaw shellfish under cold running water or thaw frozen meats and poultry by submerging them in a bowl of cold water. If submerging meats or poultry, make sure the food is sealed in a plastic bag and the cold water is refreshed every 30 minutes. With this method, 1 pound of meat or poultry will likely defrost in less than an hour. Avoid thawing frozen foods in hot water or on the counter at room temperature.

Don't forget to thoroughly wash cutting boards, knives, and any other tools that have touched raw meat before re-using them. Be especially careful not to cut produce on the same cutting board as raw meat without proper cleaning.

What is safe to put in the microwave? Glass or ceramic bowls and plates are often microwave-safe. Never use metal pans or foil in the microwave as they are fire hazards. In general, avoid using plastic, Styrofoam and melamine containers without the "microwave safe" label. There are some plastic and Styrofoam containers that are marked "microwave safe", because the FDA allows this label for containers that pass their safety standards.[12] Most take-out containers, water bottles, and plastic food tubs, such as those used for yogurt or cream cheese, are not microwave-safe. In the same way, plastic wrap should not be used to cover food in the microwave; instead, cover with a paper towel.

Cooking Temperatures

It's good practice to cook with a thermometer to ensure a proper final temperature of the food. As found in our equipment list, I highly recommend a digital instant-read thermometer, which should be used periodically during cooking to check the temperature. Be sure to take it out after checking the temperature, as this thermometer can't be kept in a heated oven or pot. Here are the minimum final cooking temperatures in degrees Fahrenheit (°F) for various foods. For more complete information on temperatures, visit FoodSafety.gov.[13]

Ground meat: 160°F

Ground chicken/turkey: 165°F

Beef (steaks) and pork: 145°F

Chicken/Turkey: 165°F

Egg dishes: 160°F

Fish: 145°F or until flesh separates with a fork

Food Storage

Cooked food can't be left out for more than two hours at room temperature. The USDA calls the temperatures from 40°F–140°F the "Danger Zone".[13] Bacteria grows rapidly in this range, which may make food unsafe. Perishable leftovers should be stored in covered containers in the refrigerator or freezer. It's best to label the container with the date and the name of what's inside. Refrigerated leftovers should be eaten within 4 days, and frozen leftovers should be eaten within 2-3 months. All leftovers should be reheated to 165°F before eating.

Check the temperature of your fridge and freezer. The fridge should be at or below 38°F, and the freezer should be at 0°F to maintain foods at their desired temperatures.

It can be tempting to thaw frozen chicken on the counter or to re-use the board you sliced raw meat on without washing it first. It's also easy to leave leftovers out too long before refrigerating them. But these practices can cause food-borne illnesses like salmonella, campylobacter, and clostridium perfringens infections. I don't say this to scare you but to empower you. Following the practices outlined in this chapter will make you more confident of the quality and safety of the food you prepare.

Stocking Your Pantry:

STAPLES AND ON-HAND INGREDIENTS

It's already 5:00pm. I worked all day, and after school my kids had soccer practice and piano lessons. I haven't even thought about dinner yet. Everyone is hungry, and I need a plan! I open my pantry to see what I can quickly make.

A strategically-stocked pantry revolutionized my cooking. With key ingredients on-hand at all times, I am encouraged to cook at home, and it makes it easier to answer the "What's for Dinner?" question. Even in my 20's, I stocked pasta, fresh garlic, canned clams, and olive oil to make a quick *Linguini with Clams* (page 93) long before I had my family to feed. Many of the recipes in this book were developed from my kitchen staples, such as *Bean and Cheese Quesadilla* (page 52), *Easy Egg Tacos* (page 45), and *30-Minute Pasta Sauce* (page 79).

So, what are these staples? This is my comprehensive list. Many of these are used in the recipes included in this book, and it's also a great place to start.

Fruits & Veggies

In this category, it's always best to pick fresh and in-season, but frozen and canned produce are good too. This is not an exhaustive list, but most of these are used in the *Kitchen Simple* recipes in the back of the book. Keep some of these fruits and vegetables at home, but you don't need to have all of these at once. Consider buying only what you will use and refer to the *Kitchen Simple* shopping lists when in the grocery store.

- *Baby Spinach, Shredded Carrots (pre-washed and ready-to-use for salads, sandwiches, wraps, and omelets)*
- *Bell Peppers, Baby Bell Peppers (green, yellow, orange or red)*
- *Tomatoes: fresh (cherry or grape, Roma) or canned (low-sodium regular diced or fire-roasted diced)*
- *Green Vegetables: broccoli, zucchini, asparagus*
- *Onions: white/yellow/sweet onions (these three types can be used interchangeably), green onions (also called scallions), red onions*
- *Mushrooms (white button, cremini/baby portobellos)*
- *Potatoes (Idaho and sweet)*
- *A Variety of Fruits (apples, bananas, oranges, grapes)*

Dairy

Yogurt and milk are perishable, so only buy what you'll eat in a week.

Hard cheeses stay fresher longer and can withstand freezing.

- *Hard Cheeses (shredded or wedged): Parmesan cheese, cheddar cheese*
- *Greek Yogurt (low-fat or fat-free): has two times the protein of regular yogurt*
- *Milk (low-fat or fat-free)*

Grains

- *Brown Rice (instant)*
- *Breakfast Cereals: whole grain (such as Kashi Go Lean or Grape Nuts)*
- *Oatmeal (regular or quick one-minute oats)*
- *Pasta: whole grain*
- *Breads or Rolls: whole grain*
- *Tortillas: whole grain*
- *Flour: whole wheat and/or brown rice flour*
- *Other: quinoa, couscous, polenta*

Protein

(rotate protein foods from this list for variety in your weekly meals)

- *Beef, Pork, and/or Turkey (lean, fresh or frozen)*
- *Chicken Breasts and Thighs (boneless and skinless, fresh or frozen)*
- *Ground Meat: beef, turkey, and/or chicken (lean, fresh or frozen)*
- *Canned Beans: kidney, cannellini, pinto, black beans, garbanzo/ chick peas*
- *Frozen Fish, Shellfish*
- *Canned Salmon, Tuna, Clams*
- *Lentils (dried or canned)*
- *Tofu*
- *Eggs*

Fats & Oils

- *Olive Oil, Canola Oil*
- *Olive Oil Cooking Spray*
- *Butter or Soft Spread Margarine (Earth Balance)*

Seasonings & Condiments

These are the on-hand ingredients as labeled in the shopping list for the *Kitchen Simple* recipes in this book. At first, you will be gradually building your pantry supply as you purchase what you need each week, but these seasonings and condiments will carry over the next time you make these recipes.

- *Ground Black Pepper*
- *Salt (iodized)*
- *Chicken Bouillon*
- *Dijon Mustard*
- *Soy Sauce*
- *Worcestershire Sauce*
- *Barbecue Sauce (refrigerate when opened)*
- *Chili Sauce (refrigerate when opened)*
- *Salsa (refrigerate when opened)*
- *Red Wine Vinegar, Balsamic Vinegar*
- *Dried Herbs and Spices: cumin, oregano, parsley, red pepper flakes, chili powder, Italian seasoning, red pepper (cayenne), bay leaves*
- *Fresh Garlic*
- *Honey and Pure Maple Syrup*

If you keep essential ingredients on-hand, you'll always have an answer when asked, "What's for dinner?" When cooking meals at home, you'll save money compared to eating out. Continue reading to find out more ways to save money in the kitchen!

Budget Wise:

HOW TO STRETCH THE DOLLAR WHEN STARTING A KITCHEN

My mom and dad had a tight food budget when they were newlyweds. A food outlet near their first apartment sold canned goods without labels for 5 cents a can. They would randomly choose an unlabeled can from the bin marked "vegetables" or the bin marked "fruits". This made every mealtime a great surprise. Mom would open a can hoping for corn or beans to compliment her meal and found sauerkraut or okra instead. Other times, she opened a can she had picked from the "fruit" bin for dessert but found it to be a vegetable instead. Don't worry, this chapter on budget won't encourage you to use such drastic cost-saving methods. Instead, it focuses on two solid budget-conscious practices you can employ in your kitchen: cooking at home and reducing food waste.

What I want to do is equip you with all you need to make cooking at home a reality. Forbes estimates you spend five times more money ordering take-out from a restaurant compared to cooking at home.[14] Even the "meal-in-a-box" kits people often subscribe to and cook at home cost approximately three times the amount you'd spend on groceries when making your own meal. The recipes in this book are quick to make and have budget-friendly items, including low-cost produce such as potatoes, celery and onions, and budget-friendly protein like eggs and canned beans.

Before you go shopping, make a grocery list (using the lists provided in the recipe sets at the end of this book) so you're not buying things you won't use. Buy only enough food for one week, and pay attention to "sell-by" and "use-by" dates. Be especially attentive to the dates on salad greens, dairy products, and packaged fresh meat and chicken. Compare them to other packages on the shelf to get the newest, freshest ingredients. When your groceries are home, organize perishables in the fridge to place the ones that expire first in prominent places in order to use them by their expiration dates.

Sometimes there's a trade-off when balancing saving time and money. For example, buying a block of cheese and grating it at home may save some money compared to purchasing cheese that is already shredded. But is this extra step worth it if it costs more of your time? I don't recommend any savings that would hinder you from making meals at home. The general rule is that cooking at home is intrinsically thrifty. So, sometimes spending a little extra for pre-shredded carrots or pre-minced garlic that saves time, and therefore increasing your likelihood to cook at home, is a wise move!

Using your freezer for more than ice cubes and ice cream can save money too. Think of it as an addition to your pantry. Many foods (including fruits, cheese, herbs, nuts/seeds, grains and bread) can be frozen to extend their shelf life. Peeled ripe bananas, rinsed and dried berries, washed grapes, and sliced peaches, pineapple, and mangoes can all be frozen and are great additions to smoothies. One of my favorite protein-packed smoothies is my recipe for *Peanut Butter Blueberry Banana Smoothie* (page 94). Frozen grapes and blueberries make refreshing snacks, too. Buying shredded cheese in bulk and putting extra cheese into a freezer bag for later is a wise money-saving option. Fresh herbs can be frozen and used any time a recipe calls for them. Cooked grains, such as rice and quinoa, can also be frozen. Portion them into smaller freezer bags to use in a rice/quinoa bowl for a future lunch. Sliced bread also lasts in the freezer. In the morning, when making your sandwich to bring to work or school, use frozen slices of bread, and they'll be thawed and fresh for lunchtime.

In general, freezing extra food helps cut down on food waste, ultimately saving money. Approximately 40% of our U.S. food supply is wasted.[15] Consumers are the largest contributor of food waste, throwing away an estimated 21% of all food purchased.[16] A family of four throws out an estimated average of $1,484 worth of edible food per year.[17] The meal plans and shopping lists you will find in this book help you buy only what you need. When you repurpose leftovers by freezing them or using them within 4 days (when stored promptly in refrigerator), you reduce food waste. Also, it helps to use ingredients before they expire. Uneaten food affects our wallets and wastes the natural resources—land, water, and energy—used to produce that food. We fill landfills with this unused food, which then releases climate-changing methane gas into our environment. All of us can have an impact on reducing food waste. When we waste less food, it's a win-win: we help our environment and save money.

You've Got This!

It was divine intervention. I was attending a national nutrition conference for some continuing education credits I needed. At that point in my career, I was considering what was next for me and praying for direction. Should I return to working in a hospital or to conducting research? Should I look for an outpatient counseling job or another corporate position? Or, should I pursue something entirely new? During the conference, I jumped into a session about blogging and social media platforms. That's when it hit me. I would combine my nutrition background and my kitchen experience to launch MyPlate2Yours. I knew first-hand that life is busy, and it's a challenge to cook and feed healthy foods to myself and my growing family. If I had trouble, I knew others did, too.

The kitchen means more to me than simply a place to make food. It is a gathering place, a nurturing place, a place for connection and conversation. It is my life's passion to share with others the love I have for the kitchen and all that it holds. It's my sincere privilege to share my knowledge and experience with you.

Now it is time to put all of what we've just covered into practice. You can begin with the menus and recipes found in this next section called "Kitchen Simple". There are four sets of recipes, each with their own shopping lists: Original, Vegetarian, Protein, and Variety. Each set of recipes contains 7 different meals that can be used for lunches and dinners. The best part about each set is that a week of meals are created from a total of 15 ingredients, in addition to the kitchen staples you have on-hand (these are the seasonings and condiments recommended in Chapter 5, "Stocking Your Pantry: Staples and On-Hand Ingredients"). If you don't plan on making all the meals in the set, adjust the shopping list accordingly. With 7 recipes from only 15 ingredients, grocery shopping for the week will be a breeze!

Original is the starting point. These are the most basic set of recipes in this collection. **Vegetarian** offers recipes featuring plant protein from beans and lentils. **Protein** recipes utilize chicken thighs and ground meats (you pick: beef, chicken or turkey). And **Variety** recipes gently begin introducing a few new concepts to try as you gain confidence in the kitchen.

Now it's time to unleash *your* potential in your kitchen. Each of us can write our own stories about our adventurous culinary pursuits. My hope is that your story starts now and that with your new-found knowledge, you'll have great success. Now you know exactly where to begin: this is Not Your Mama's Kitchen!

CHAPTER 8

Kitchen Simple Recipes & Shopping Lists:

FOUR SETS OF 7 RECIPES WITH 15 INGREDIENTS

A MONTH OF MEALS!

Original

A collection of 7 tasty recipes featuring 13 main ingredients

1 CHICKEN STIR FRY

2 PASTA SALAD WITH CHICKEN & VEGGIES

3 POTATO AND EGG BAKE

4 EASY EGG TACOS

5 VEGGIE PASTA BOWL

6 CHEDDAR CHICKEN & POTATO PACKETS

7 ENTRÉE SPINACH SALAD

ORIGINAL SHOPPING LIST

Grains
 1 small package whole grain tortillas
 1 box (14 ounces) Minute brown rice
 1 pound whole grain pasta

Produce
 10 ounces baby spinach
 3 Idaho potatoes
 1 package shredded carrots
 1 package baby bell peppers
 2 large onions (white, yellow or sweet)

Protein
 ½ dozen eggs
 2 pounds boneless, skinless chicken breast

Dairy
 1 cup low-fat or fat-free plain Greek yogurt
 2 ½ cups shredded cheddar cheese

Grocery
 1 can (15 ounces) cannellini beans

Kitchen Staples
 Salt & pepper
 Olive oil
 BBQ sauce
 Dijon mustard
 Soy sauce
 Honey
 Garlic
 Red wine vinegar
 Red pepper flakes

⤳ ORIGINAL RECIPES ⤳

1 Chicken Stir Fry (serves 2-3)

Check it out! A quick, step-by-step video on how to make this recipe is available on myplate2yours.com.

Ingredients

¾ pound boneless, skinless chicken breast, cut into ½-inch strips

2 tablespoons oil, separate

2 cloves garlic, minced

4 mini yellow bell peppers, cut into strips (the size of matchsticks)

½ cup shredded carrots

¼ cup sliced onion

1 handful baby spinach

¼ cup soy sauce mixed with 2 teaspoons honey

2-3 servings Minute brown rice, prepared according to package directions

Directions

1. Heat 1 tablespoon oil in skillet over medium-high heat. Quickly stir in garlic to lightly brown.

2. Add chicken strips. Cook until lightly brown, moving the chicken pieces with a spatula until no pink remains in middle. Remove chicken from pan onto a plate.

3. Add another tablespoon of oil to the pan. When hot, add onions, peppers and carrots. Using a spatula, sauté veggies by quickly moving them around in the hot skillet until tender crisp, about 3-5 minutes.

4. Return chicken to pan and add spinach. Sauté until spinach wilts.

5. Stir the soy sauce/honey mixture and add to pan. Sauté to heat sauce.

6. Serve over rice. Enjoy!

2 Pasta Salad with Chicken & Veggies

(serves 1-2)

Ingredients

½ pound whole-grain pasta, cooked according to directions

½ pound chicken breast, poached* and diced

4 baby bell peppers, diced

¼ onion, diced

¼ cup shredded carrots

1 clove garlic, diced

½ cup shredded cheese

Dressing:

3 tablespoons olive oil

3 tablespoons red wine vinegar

1 teaspoon Dijon mustard

1 pinch salt

Directions

1. Mix dressing ingredients in a small jar. Seal with a lid and shake to combine. Set aside.

2. In a medium bowl, combine pasta, chicken, bell pepper, onion, carrots, garlic and cheese.

3. Add dressing and mix to combine.

4. Chill in the refrigerator until ready to serve. Enjoy!

*Refer to chapter 3 for instructions on how to poach chicken.

3 Potato and Egg Bake (serves 2)

Ingredients

2 large potatoes, washed and pricked with fork 4 times

2 eggs

1 tablespoon olive oil

¼ cup shredded cheddar cheese

¼ cup onion, diced

½ cup baby spinach, chopped

Salt and ground black pepper, to taste

Red pepper flakes

Foil sheet

Directions

1. Place potatoes in microwave and cook on high until potatoes are soft, 8-10 minutes.

2. Meanwhile, preheat oven to 400°F. Prepare a baking sheet with parchment paper. Set aside.

3. Prepare potatoes for stuffing by cutting off a thin layer from top of each potato, lengthwise. Place potatoes on prepared baking sheet.

4. Hollow out the potatoes by scooping out a large spoonful of flesh. Reserve this potato flesh by placing it on top of each cut potato skin.

5. Brush both potatoes and reserve potato flesh lightly with olive oil. Season with salt, pepper and red pepper flakes.

6. Add half of the diced onions, spinach and shredded cheese to each hollowed potato.

7. Crack an egg into each potato. Top potatoes with reserved potato flesh and skin. Season with salt and pepper, if desired.

8. Cook stuffed potatoes for 20 minutes or until egg whites are set and yolk is soft. Enjoy!

Recipe inspired by www.ourbestbites.com

4 Easy Egg Tacos (serves 2)

Check it out! A quick, step-by-step video on how to make this recipe is available on myplate2yours.com.

Ingredients

2-3 eggs

2 tablespoons onion, diced

4 mini bell peppers, sliced thin and quartered

2 teaspoons olive oil

Salt and ground black pepper, to taste

¼ cup shredded cheddar cheese

2 whole grain tortillas

Directions

1. Crack eggs into small bowl. Whisk to blend.

2. Heat oil in a skillet over medium-high heat. Sauté bell peppers with onions, 3-5 minutes.

3. Pour eggs over veggies. Using a spatula, scramble eggs by occasionally moving eggs around in skillet until eggs glisten but are no longer runny, 2-3 minutes. Turn off heat.

4. Sprinkle eggs with shredded cheese. Serve eggs immediately on warmed tortillas*.

5. Garnish with salsa. Enjoy!

*Warmed Tortillas

Tortillas can be made in a separate small skillet on the cooktop. Add 1 tortilla and heat for 1-2 minutes. Flip with tongs and heat second side for 1 minute. Remove and repeat to heat second tortilla.

Tortillas can also be warmed in a microwave: wrap the tortillas with a paper towel and place on a microwave-safe plate. Heat for 10-15 seconds.

5 Veggie Pasta Bowl (serves 2)

Ingredients

½ pound pasta, prepare according to package directions

1 tablespoon olive oil

1 clove garlic, minced

2-3 baby bell peppers, sliced

¼ onion, sliced thin

¼ cup shredded carrots

Fresh spinach, generous handful

½ cup cannellini beans

½ cup shredded cheese

Directions

1. Prepare beans by opening the cans with a can opener. Place a colander in kitchen sink and pour beans into it. Rinse beans with water and allow them to drain completely. Reserve ½ cup beans for recipe and store remainder in covered container in the refrigerator (to use in the Entrée Spinach Salad).

2. Using a skillet, heat olive oil over medium-high heat. Sauté veggies with garlic in olive oil until tender crisp.

3. Add ½ cup cannellini beans. Remove skillet from heat.

4. Place cooked pasta in serving bowl. Add contents of skillet and gently combine.

5. Top with shredded cheese. Enjoy!

This recipe is very flexible with ingredients. Feel free to include any veggies you have 'on hand' or add diced poached chicken for extra protein.

6 Cheddar Chicken & Potato Packets

(serves 2)

Check it out! This recipe is featured on Dinner Tonight (a live cooking session in Lynn's kitchen) at myplate2yours.com/videos.

Ingredients

2 tablespoons BBQ sauce

2 small (3 ounces each) boneless, skinless chicken breasts

1 potato, unpeeled, sliced thin

4 red baby bell pepper, sliced into thin strips

½ onion, sliced very thin

Salt and ground black pepper

½ cup cheddar cheese, shredded

2 tablespoons plain Greek yogurt

Directions

1. Preheat oven to 375°F.

2. Place individual foil sheets on flat surface. Add ½ tablespoon BBQ sauce in center of each foil sheet.

3. Place a chicken breast on top of sauce. Spread another ½ tablespoon on both chicken breasts.

4. Cover each chicken breast with ½ of the potato, 2 or 3 strips bell pepper, and 2 or 3 slices onion. Sprinkle with salt and pepper.

5. Make foil packets: match opposite corners together and roll down to secure. Secure open ends by folding to enclose while leaving interior space for food to steam.

6. Place packets on a baking sheet and bake in oven for 30 minutes.

7. Remove from oven and carefully open packets. Sprinkle ¼ cup shredded cheese on each.

8. Return to oven, unsealed, for about 3 minutes until cheese melts and chicken is 165°F.

9. Transfer to serving plates and garnish with plain Greek yogurt (or low-fat sour cream). Enjoy!

Recipe adapted from MidwestDairy.com

7 Entrée Spinach Salad (serves 2)

Ingredients

4 cups fresh baby spinach (5 ounces)

¼ onion, sliced thin

¼ cup shredded carrots

¼ cup cannellini beans

2 hard boiled eggs*, peeled and quartered

Dressing:

¼ cup olive oil

2 tablespoons red wine vinegar

1 teaspoon Dijon mustard

¼ teaspoon salt

⅛ teaspoon pepper

Directions

1. Combine dressing ingredients in a small jar with a lid. Shake well.
2. Place spinach on a serving plate.
3. Arrange onion, carrots, beans and sliced egg on top.
4. Drizzle salad dressing on top and lightly toss. Enjoy!

Need something more for dinner in addition to the salad? Try making a quick quesadilla: place tortilla on small microwavable plate. Sprinkle desired amount of shredded cheddar cheese on a tortilla, fold and heat in microwave for 30-45 seconds until the cheese melts.

Vegetarian

A collection of 7 tasty recipes featuring 15 main ingredients

1 BEAN AND CHEESE QUESADILLA

2 LENTIL PORTOBELLO MARINARA

3 FIESTA TOSTADA

4 BLACK BEAN CAKES WITH SPICY YOGURT SAUCE

5 GRILLED CHEDDAR CHEESE AND APPLE SANDWICH

6 NAKED BEAN AND RICE BURRITO

7 WARM SWEET POTATO, LENTIL AND APPLE BOWL

VEGETARIAN SHOPPING LIST

Grains

1 package (4-8 count) whole grain tortillas

1 box (14 ounces) Minute brown rice

1 loaf whole wheat bread

Produce

3 apples (Granny Smith or Gala)

1 package shredded carrots

2 red bell peppers

2 onions (white, yellow or sweet)

1 pound cremini (also known as baby porto-bello) mushrooms

2 pounds sweet potatoes

2 stalks celery (optional)

Protein

2 cans (15 ounces each) pinto beans

1 can (15 ounces) black beans

1 can (15 ounces) lentils (or small package dried lentils)

Dairy

1 cup low-fat or fat-free plain Greek yogurt

2 cups shredded cheddar cheese

Grocery

1 can (15 ounces) fire-roasted diced tomatoes

1 can (15 ounces) sweet corn

Kitchen Staples

Salt & pepper

Olive oil

Garlic

Red wine vinegar

Red pepper flakes

Salsa

Honey

Bay leaves

Cumin

Chili powder

Butter

Olive oil cooking spray

⇒ VEGETARIAN RECIPES ⇒

1 Bean and Cheese Quesadilla (serves 2)

Check it out! A quick, step-by-step video on how to make this recipe is available on myplate2yours.com.

Ingredients

2 whole-grain soft tortillas

½ cup pinto beans, rinsed and drained

½ cup shredded sharp cheddar cheese

Directions

1. Preheat oven to 350°F.

2. In a small bowl, mash beans with a fork.

3. Spread the beans on each of the two tortillas. Sprinkle with cheese.

4. Place on a baking sheet and cook in oven for 10 minutes (until cheese is bubbly and browning begins).

5. When removed from the oven, place on a cutting board. Fold each in half and cut into 3 or 4 triangle pieces with a chef knife. Serve with salsa and enjoy!

Easy adds (these ingredients can be added before cheese is sprinkled): cooked chicken or shrimp, onions, tomatoes, avocado and/or spinach.

2 **Lentil Portobello Marinara** (serves 2)

Ingredients

¼ cup olive oil

½ small onion, diced

1 garlic clove, minced

½ cup shredded carrots, chopped

½ cup baby portobello/cremini mushrooms, chopped (about ¼ pound)

1 stalk celery, diced (optional)

1 can (15 ounces) fire-roasted diced tomatoes (undrained)

1 tablespoon red wine vinegar

1 bay leaf

1 teaspoon dried basil

1 tablespoon honey

Salt and ground black pepper, to taste

1 cup cooked lentils*

2 servings Minute brown rice, prepared according to package directions

Directions

1. Heat oil on medium heat in a saucepan. Add onions and garlic, cook until onions are translucent.

2. Add all other ingredients to pan except the honey, lentils, and salt and pepper. Bring to a boil, reduce heat and gently simmer uncovered for 30-45 minutes, until sauce thickens. Remove from heat.

3. Add lentils and honey. Season with salt and pepper. Serve on prepared Minute rice. Enjoy!

*Cooked Lentils

Canned lentils are cooked. You'll need to drain and rinse them before using.

If using dried lentils, prepare them by filling a saucepan with water. Heat water until boiling and add ½ (for 1 cup cooked) or ¼ cup (for ½ cup cooked) of dry lentils. Reduce heat to gentle simmer and cook until tender, 5-10 minutes. Drain in colander. Do not overcook—lentils become mushy if overcooked.

3 **Fiesta Tostada** (serves 2)

Ingredients

2 tortillas

½ cup corn

½ cup pinto beans

¼ cup shredded carrots

1 red bell pepper (about ½ cup)

¼ cup olive oil

2 tablespoon red wine vinegar

Salsa and plain Greek yogurt for garnish

Olive oil cooking spray

Salt and ground black pepper

Directions

1. Preheat oven to 400°F.
2. Prepare tortillas with a light coat of cooking spray on both sides. Place on baking sheet. Sprinkle tops with salt.
3. Bake 3-5 minutes, until tortillas are crispy and light golden color. Turn tortillas over and bake again, 3-5 minutes.
4. Meanwhile, mix corn, beans, carrots and bell peppers in a bowl. Add oil and vinegar. Season with salt and pepper.
5. When shells are ready, top with equal amounts of bean and corn mix. Garnish with salsa and plain Greek yogurt. Enjoy!

4 Black Bean Cakes with Spicy Yogurt Sauce (makes 10 small cakes)

Check it out! A quick, step-by-step video on how to make this recipe is available on myplate2yours.com.

Ingredients

1 tablespoon olive oil

1 small onion, diced

3 cloves garlic, minced

1 small (or ½ large) red bell pepper, diced

½ cup chopped cremini/baby portobello mushrooms (about ¼ pound)

1 small sweet potato, peeled and grated (about ½ cup)

1 teaspoon cumin

1 teaspoon chili powder

1 can (15 ounces) black beans, rinsed and drained

½ cup whole wheat bread crumbs (can be made by toasting a slice of bread, placing it in a quart-size Ziploc bag on a counter, and hitting it with a saucepan until crumbs form)

½ cup water

Spicy Yogurt Dip

1 cup plain Greek yogurt

1 garlic clove, minced

¼ teaspoon cumin

½ teaspoon salt

Directions

1. In a small bowl, mix Spicy Yogurt Dip ingredients thoroughly and chill in the refrigerator.

2. Preheat oven to 500°F.

3. Lightly coat baking sheet with cooking spray. Set aside.

4. Heat oil in a skillet and sauté onion, garlic, and bell pepper for 3 minutes, until onion is translucent.

5. Stir in cumin and chili powder. Heat until spices are fragrant.

6. Add mushrooms and sweet potato to hot pan and stir to cook until mushrooms are soft. Remove from heat.

7. Place beans in a medium bowl and roughly mash with a large fork. Add contents of skillet to beans and combine. Sprinkle in breadcrumbs and pour in water. Stir again to combine.

8. Divide mixture in half and make 5 equal cakes from each half (10 total). Place on baking sheet.

9. Lightly coat bean cakes with oil. Place in middle of oven and bake for 5 minutes until cake tops begin to crisp. Flip and bake 5 minutes more (when second side gets crispy). 10. Serve on a platter with a dollop of Spicy Yogurt Sauce. Enjoy! *Make these into sandwiches on sliced bread! Leftover black bean cakes can be stored in a sealed container in the refrigerator for up to 4 days or the freezer for up to 3 months.*

5 Grilled Cheddar Cheese and Apple Sandwich (serves 2)

Ingredients

4 slices whole wheat bread

⅔ cup shredded sharp cheddar cheese

2 teaspoons of butter (½ of teaspoon for each slice of bread)

1 apple (Granny Smith or Gala), thinly sliced

Directions

1. Lightly butter one side of each piece of bread.

2. Put the bread, buttered side facing down, in a skillet over medium heat.

3. Place ⅓ cup cheese on top of 2 pieces of bread and cover with 2-4 slices of apples.

4. Top these with the unbuttered side of remaining toasted bread slices.

5. Cook for about 1 minute on each side or until cheese melts and the sides of the bread become lightly brown.

6. Remove from heat, slice in half and it is ready to eat. Enjoy!

6 Naked Bean and Rice Burrito (serves 2)

Ingredients

1 can (15 ounces) pinto beans

1 can (15 ounces) sweet corn, drained in colander

½ cup shredded sharp cheddar cheese

2 cups cooked Minute brown rice (prepared from 1 cup dry)

Toppings: salsa & plain Greek yogurt

Directions

1. Prepare beans by opening the cans with a can opener. Place a colander in kitchen sink and pour beans into it. Rinse beans with water and allow them to drain completely.

2. Meanwhile prepare rice according to package directions for 2 servings.

3. Divide hot rice between 2 bowls.

4. Place ½ cup beans, ½ cup corn, and ¼ cup cheese onto each rice bowl. Top with your choice of salsa and toppings. Enjoy!

7 Warm Sweet Potato, Lentil and Apple Bowl (serves 2)

Ingredients

1 tablespoon olive oil

1 pound sweet potatoes, peeled and diced (about 1-inch cubes)

½ small onion, diced (large dices)

2 teaspoons fresh rosemary (or ½ teaspoon dried)

Salt and ground black pepper

4 ounces cremini/baby portobello mushrooms, sliced

1 clove garlic, minced

2 small apples (Granny Smith or Gala), diced

1 stalk celery, sliced (optional)

½ cup cooked lentils*

Directions

1. Preheat oven 425°F.

2. Place potatoes and onions on baking sheet and toss with ½ tablespoon olive oil. Sprinkle with rosemary, salt and pepper.

3. Place high in oven to roast for 20 minutes, until tender.

4. Meanwhile, heat ½ tablespoon oil in a skillet over medium heat. Sauté mushrooms, garlic and celery until mushrooms and celery are softened.

5. Season with salt and pepper, to taste.

6. Add apples and cook until just warm.

7. Pour contents of the skillet into a large bowl. Add roasted potatoes and onions to bowl.

8. Gently stir in lentils to combine all ingredients.

9. Divide into two bowls to serve. Enjoy!

*Cooked Lentils

Canned lentils are cooked. You'll need to drain and rinse them before using.
If using dried lentils, prepare them by filling a saucepan with water. Heat water until boiling and add ½ (for 1 cup cooked) or ¼ cup (for ½ cup cooked) of dry lentils. Reduce heat to gentle simmer and cook until tender, 5-10 minutes. Drain in colander. Do not overcook—lentils become mushy if overcooked.

Protein

A collection of 7 tasty recipes featuring 15 main ingredients

1 CHEESY MEAT AND TOMATO PASTA SKILLET

2 OVEN-BAKED ITALIAN SLIDERS

3 HEARTY CHILI

4 LEMON CHICKEN AND POTATO PACKETS

5 CREAMY STROGANOFF

6 SHEET PAN ITALIAN CHICKEN WITH VEGETABLES

7 SPICY ORANGE CHICKEN THIGHS

PROTEIN SHOPPING LIST

Grains

- 8 whole-grain slider buns
- 1 package egg noodles

Produce

- 6 medium onions (white, yellow or sweet)
- 1 medium zucchini
- 3 Idaho potatoes
- 1 pound mushrooms (white button)
- 2 green bell peppers

Protein

- 1 egg
- 2 pounds boneless, skinless chicken thighs
- 3 ½ pounds 85-90% lean ground beef or ground turkey

Dairy

- ¾ cup Parmesan cheese
- 1 cup low-fat or fat-free plain Greek yogurt

Grocery

- ½ cup orange juice
- 3 cans (15 ounces each) fire-roasted diced tomatoes
- 1 can (15 ounces) kidney beans

Kitchen Staples

- Salt & pepper
- Olive oil
- Dried oregano
- Garlic
- Lemon juice (from fresh lemon)
- Italian seasoning
- Chili powder
- Worcestershire sauce
- Red pepper (cayenne)
- Maple syrup
- Chili sauce

⤜ PROTEIN RECIPES ⤛

For the recipes that serve 4, save half of the finished recipe in the fridge for lunch in the next 3-4 days or freeze in a sealed container to be defrosted and reheated for a future dinner.

1 Cheesy Meat and Tomato Pasta Skillet (serves 4)

Check it out! A quick, step-by-step video on how to make this recipe is available on myplate2yours.com.

Ingredients

- 1 pound lean ground meat
- 1 medium onion, chopped
- 1 clove garlic, minced
- ½ teaspoon salt
- 1 can (15 ounces) fire-roasted diced tomatoes (do not drain)
- 1 teaspoon Italian seasoning
- ⅛ teaspoon ground red pepper
- 1 medium zucchini, cut into ½-inch thick slices
- 1 ½ cups uncooked egg noodles
- ¼ cup grated Parmesan cheese

Directions

1. In a skillet, brown ground beef, onion, and garlic over medium heat for 8-10 minutes or until beef is no longer pink, breaking into crumbles. Remove beef onto a plate with a slotted spoon; pour off drippings (into a paper cup that will be discarded). Season meat with salt and set aside.

2. In the same skillet, add tomatoes, Italian seasoning, red pepper, zucchini and egg noodles. Fill the empty tomato can with water (15 ounces) and add to skillet.

3. Push pasta into liquid to submerge. Bring to a boil; then reduce heat and simmer, uncovered for 10-15 minutes until pasta is tender, stirring occasionally.

4. Return beef to skillet and heat through. Sprinkle dish with cheese and serve. Enjoy!

2 **Oven-Baked Italian Sliders** (serves 2)

Ingredients

½ pound lean ground meat

1 egg

2 tablespoons whole-wheat bread crumbs (can be made by toasting a whole-grain bun, placing in a quart-size Ziploc bag on a counter, and hitting it with a saucepan until crumbs form)

2 teaspoons shredded Parmesan cheese

1 clove garlic, minced

½ teaspoon Italian seasoning

½ teaspoon salt

Ground black pepper

4 whole-grain slider buns or dinner rolls

Directions

1. Preheat oven to 350°F.

2. Combine all ingredients in a medium bowl until they are well-mixed.

3. Form mixture into 4 patties, each about 3 inches in diameter. Place patties on a greased baking sheet (or one lined with parchment paper).

4. Bake for 8 minutes. Flip patties and bake 8-10 minutes more.

5. Serve on a whole-grain slider bun or dinner roll. Top with marinara sauce or ketchup and lettuce, tomato and/or onion. Enjoy!

3 **Hearty Chili** (serves 4)

Ingredients

1 pound lean ground meat

1 can (15 ounces) kidney beans, drained and rinsed

2 garlic cloves, minced

1 medium onion, diced

1 green pepper, diced

2-3 tablespoons chili powder

2 cans (15 ounces each) fire-roasted diced tomatoes (do not drain)

2 teaspoons Worcestershire sauce

½ teaspoon salt

Directions

1. Prepare beans by opening the cans with a can opener. Place a colander in kitchen sink and pour beans into it. Rinse beans with water and allow them to drain completely. Set aside.

2. In a saucepan, cook ground meat over medium high heat until light brown. Remove meat with a slotted spoon; pour off drippings (into a paper cup that will be discarded).

3. Return meat to the skillet with medium heat, and add garlic, onion, and green pepper.

4. Cook and stir to start softening veggies, 2-3 minutes. Add chili powder and cook and stir a few minutes more.

5. Add canned tomatoes, sauce, Worcestershire, beans and salt.

6. Gently simmer uncovered for 30-40 minutes. Enjoy!

4 Lemon Chicken and Potato Packets

(serves 2)

Check it out! A quick, step-by-step video on how to make this recipe is available on myplate2yours.com.

Ingredients

½ pound boneless, skinless chicken thighs, cut into 1-inch cubes

½ pound Yukon Gold potatoes, cut into ½-inch cubes

½ medium onion, diced

1 small zucchini, diced

½ green bell pepper, diced

1 tablespoon olive oil

1 tablespoon lemon juice

1 teaspoon Italian seasoning

1 garlic clove, minced

½ teaspoon salt

¼ cup of shredded Parmesan cheese

Directions

1. Preheat oven to 400°F.

2. Mix all ingredients together except Parmesan cheese.

3. Place equal amounts onto 2 large squares of foil.

4. Make foil packets: match opposite corners together and roll down to secure. Secure open ends by folding to enclose while leaving interior space for food to steam.

5. Place packets on baking sheet. Bake for 30 minutes until chicken is cooked (165°F) and potatoes are soft.

6. Carefully open packets and sprinkle equal amounts of Parmesan over each. Enjoy!

5 Creamy Stroganoff (serves 4)

Ingredients

- 1 pound lean ground meat
- ½ pound white button mushrooms, wiped clean with a paper towel and sliced
- 1 medium onion, chopped
- ⅓ cup chili sauce
- 1 teaspoon Worcestershire sauce
- 1 teaspoon salt
- ½ teaspoon ground black pepper
- 1 cup plain Greek yogurt
- ½ pound egg noodles, prepared according to package directions

Directions

1. Brown ground meat in a skillet. Remove beef with a slotted spoon; pour off drippings (into a paper cup that will be discarded).

2. Return meat to skillet and with medium-high heat, add mushrooms and onion. Cook until onion is soft and translucent.

3. Stir in chili sauce, Worcestershire, salt, and pepper.

4. Just before serving, stir in yogurt. Serve over cooked egg noodles. Enjoy!

This dish goes well with sautéed zucchini or a side salad.

6 Sheet Pan Italian Chicken with Vegetables (serves 2)

Check it out! This recipe is featured on Dinner Tonight (a live cooking session in Lynn's kitchen) at myplate2yours.com/videos.

Ingredients

2 boneless, skinless chicken thighs (1 pound maximum)

2 potatoes, peeled and sliced into ½-inch wedges

1 large onion, quartered

¼ pound white button mushrooms, wipe clean with paper towel and keep whole

2 tablespoons olive oil

½ tablespoon Italian seasoning

2 cloves garlic, minced

¼ teaspoon salt

¼ teaspoon ground black pepper

Directions

1. Preheat oven to 425°F.

2. Mix oil, oregano, garlic, salt and pepper in a small bowl.

3. Cover baking sheet with aluminum foil. Place chicken and vegetables on rimmed baking sheet.

4. Pour oil & seasonings over chicken and vegetables. Move ingredients around on pan for all to be coated with oil and in a single layer on pan.

5. Place baking sheet high in oven to roast for 30-35 minutes (until internal temperature of chicken is 165°F). Enjoy!

7 Spicy Orange Chicken Thighs (serves 2)

Check it out! This recipe is featured on Dinner Tonight (a live cooking session in Lynn's kitchen) at myplate2yours.com/videos.

Ingredients

2 boneless, skinless chicken thighs (1 pound maximum)

½ cup orange juice

¼ cup pure maple syrup

⅛ teaspoon red pepper

½ teaspoon salt

½ teaspoon ground black pepper

1 tablespoons olive oil

4 ounces egg noodles, prepared according to package directions (makes 2 cups cooked)

Directions

1. In a saucepan, bring orange juice to a boil. Reduce heat slightly to keep at a low boil for 5 minutes. Stir occasionally.

2. Stir in maple syrup and red pepper. Continue to boil for another 5 minutes (until original total volume is reduced by half and it begins to thicken).

3. Meanwhile, sprinkle salt and black pepper on chicken thighs. In a skillet, heat olive oil over medium heat. Add chicken to pan, cover and sauté for 5 minutes until chicken is lightly browned.

4. Using tongs, flip chicken over and pour maple orange mixture over chicken. Reduce heat to simmer, cover, and let cook for 10-15 minutes or until chicken is cooked through (165°F).

5. To serve, portion egg noodles onto 2 plates and top with chicken and a few spoonfuls of glaze. Enjoy!

This dish matches well with steamed broccoli or roasted asparagus. Either of these can be prepared while the chicken is simmering in step 4.

Variety

A collection of 7 tasty recipes featuring 15 main ingredients

1 STUFFED GREEN PEPPERS

2 30-MINUTE WHITE TURKEY CHILI

3 30-MINUTE PASTA SAUCE

4 EASY CHICKEN CACCIATORE

5 ITALIAN CHICKEN AND ORZO SOUP

6 ORZO SALAD WITH CANNELLINI BEANS AND HOMEMADE VINAIGRETTE

7 TURKEY KEBABS ON BED OF SPINACH

VARIETY SHOPPING LIST

Grains

- 1 box (14 ounces) Minute Brown Rice
- 1-2 pounds orzo pasta

Produce

- 1 package shredded carrots
- 4 green bell peppers
- 6 onions (white, yellow or sweet)
- 4 stalks celery
- 2 cups grape (or cherry) tomatoes
- 6 ounces (6 cups) baby spinach

Protein

- 2 cans (15 ounces each) cannellini beans
- 3 pounds ground turkey
- 2 pounds boneless, skinless chicken breasts

Dairy

- 6 ounces (1 ½ cups) shredded Parmesan cheese
- 4 ounces crumbled feta cheese

Grocery

- 4 cans (15 ounces each) diced tomatoes
- 2 cans (15 ounces each) tomato sauce

Kitchen Staples

- Salt & pepper
- Olive oil
- Garlic
- Red wine vinegar
- Chicken bouillon
- Bay leaves
- Cumin
- Dried parsley (if fresh not available)
- Dried oregano
- Honey

Optional:

- Ground red pepper (cayenne)
- Bamboo skewers
- Fresh parsley (1 bunch)
- Red wine (¼ cup)

VARIETY RECIPES

For the recipes that serve 4, save half of the finished recipe in the fridge for lunch in the next 3-4 days or freeze in a sealed container for a future dinner when defrosted and reheated.

1 Stuffed Green Peppers (serves 2-4)

Ingredients

2 green peppers, halved with seeds removed

1 pound ground turkey

½ cup Minute brown rice

1 small onion, finely diced, divided

1 stalk celery, finely diced

1 can (15 ounces) tomato sauce

1 teaspoon dried oregano

½ teaspoon salt

¼ teaspoon black pepper

1 clove garlic, minced

¼ cup chopped fresh parsley (or 1 ½ tablespoons dried parsley)

¼ cup shredded Parmesan cheese

Directions

1. Place green peppers, cut side down, in a Pyrex baking dish. Fill with a ½-inch deep layer of water. Cover with a dish towel and place in microwave. Cook 5 minutes or until pepper is softened. Carefully drain water from dish and flip peppers.
2. Meanwhile, preheat oven to 350° F.
3. In a medium bowl, mix together ground meat, rice, egg, salt & pepper, ½ onion, celery and ¼ cup tomato sauce. Equally divide the mixture amongst the 4 pepper halves and fill each half.
4. In a small bowl (or the tomato sauce can), combine the remaining tomato sauce, ½ onion, garlic, oregano, and parsley. Pour about 1 tablespoon of sauce on top of each pepper and the remaining sauce around peppers.
5. Add ¼ cup water to emptied tomato bowl or can, swirl to capture any tomato 'residue' and add to baking dish (around the peppers).
6. Cover baking dish with aluminum foil and place in middle of oven for 30 minutes.
7. Uncover, spoon some sauce over the peppers and sprinkle with cheese.
8. Bake for another 10 minutes, until internal temperature of ground turkey is 165°F. Enjoy!

2 30-minute White Turkey Chili (serves 4)

Check it out! This recipe is featured on Dinner Tonight (a live cooking session in Lynn's kitchen) at myplate2yours.com/videos.

Ingredients

1 pound ground turkey

1 can (15 ounces) cannellini beans, rinsed and drained

1 small onion, diced

1 green bell pepper, diced

2 cups water

2 cubes chicken bouillon

1 teaspoon dried oregano

1 teaspoon ground cumin

1 teaspoon salt

½ teaspoon ground black pepper

¼ teaspoon ground cayenne pepper (optional)

Shredded Parmesan cheese, for garnish

Directions

1. In a saucepan, cook ground turkey, onion, and bell pepper until turkey is browned and vegetables begin to soften, about 10 minutes. You do not need any additional oil to cook.

2. Stir in beans, broth and seasonings. Bring contents to a simmer and cook for 20 minutes.

3. Serve into bowls and garnish with shredded cheese. Enjoy!

3 30-Minute Pasta Sauce (serves 2-3)

Ingredients

¼ cup olive oil

1 medium onion, finely diced

¼ cup shredded carrots, finely chopped

4 cloves garlic, minced

2 cans (15 ounces each) diced tomatoes (undrained)

1 tablespoon chopped fresh parsley (or 1 teaspoon dried)

2 teaspoons honey

1 teaspoon salt

Ground black pepper

Shredded parmesan cheese, for garish

Directions

1. Heat oil in saucepan. Add onion, carrots and garlic, lower heat and cover for 5 minutes.

2. Add tomatoes, parsley, honey, salt and pepper. Simmer for 20 minutes. This is a great time to start cooking your pasta or rice.

3. The finished sauce is chunky. If a smoother texture is desired and a stand blender is available, blend to puree. Be careful when blending hot pasta sauce and work in small batches.

4. Serve on top of pasta or rice and garnish with shredded Parmesan cheese. Enjoy!

4 **Easy Chicken Cacciatore** (serves 4)

Ingredients

1 pound boneless, skinless chicken breasts

1 tablespoon olive oil

1 small onion, sliced into thin wedges

1 garlic clove, minced

1 green bell pepper, cut into ½-inch strips

Salt and ground black pepper

1 can (15 ounces) diced tomatoes (undrained)

1 can (15 ounces) tomato sauce

¼ cup red wine (optional)

2 bay leaves

½ pound cooked pasta, cooked as directed

Shredded Parmesan cheese, for garnish

Directions

1. Season chicken with salt and pepper.

2. Heat oil in a skillet. Add the chicken and brown on one side for 2-3 minutes. Using tongs, flip chicken over to brown the other side for 2-3 minutes.

3. Add garlic, onion, and bell pepper to pan. Sauté vegetables briefly, scraping the pan for any remnants of cooked chicken.

4. Add diced tomatoes, tomato sauce, bay leaves and wine, if using. Heat to slight boil, then reduce the heat and cover with a lid. Simmer the chicken for 20-30 minutes, until internal temperature is 165°F.

5. Serve over cooked pasta, if desired. Garnish with shredded Parmesan cheese. Enjoy!

5 Italian Chicken and Orzo Soup (serves 2)

Ingredients

1 tablespoon olive oil

1 pound boneless, skinless chicken breast

1 teaspoon dried oregano

1 small onion, diced

2 stalks celery, sliced

4 cloves garlic, minced

6 cups water

4 cubes chicken bouillon

½ teaspoon salt

Ground black pepper

1 can (15 ounces) diced tomatoes (undrained)

2 tablespoons fresh parsley, chopped (or 2 teaspoons dried parsley)

1 cup orzo pasta

3 cups baby spinach

Shredded Parmesan cheese, for garnish

Directions

1. Heat oil in a saucepan.

2. Sauté onion and celery until onion is translucent.

3. Add oregano and garlic; cook for a few minutes, until fragrant.

4. Sprinkle in salt and several grinds of fresh pepper.

5. Add chicken, stock, water, and tomatoes. When brought to a boil, reduce heat and simmer (partially covered) for 30 minutes.

6. Remove chicken to a plate and shred with fork.

7. Meanwhile, add the orzo and bring to a gentle boil for 10 minutes.

8. When pasta is done, return chicken to pot and add parsley and spinach. Cook until spinach is wilted. Season with salt and pepper, to taste.

9. Serve into bowls and top with shredded Parmesan cheese. Enjoy!

6 Orzo Salad with Cannellini Beans and Homemade Vinaigrette (serves 4)

Ingredients

½ pound orzo pasta, cooked according to package directions

½ can cannellini beans, rinsed and drained

1 cup cherry tomatoes, halved (or quartered, if large)

1 cup baby spinach, chopped

1 stalk celery, diced

2 tablespoons onion, diced

2 ounces feta cheese (about ⅓ cup)

Homemade Vinaigrette:

¼ cup red wine vinegar

½ cup olive oil

½ teaspoon salt

½ teaspoon ground black pepper

½ teaspoon dried oregano

Directions

1. In a pint-size jar with a lid, combine ingredients for Homemade Vinaigrette. Seal jar and shake to combine. Set aside.

2. In a large bowl, combine all salad ingredients, except cheese and dressing.

3. Use desired quantity of Homemade Vinaigrette on salad and save remaining dressing in sealed jar in the refrigerator.

4. Add feta cheese to salad bowl and gently toss.

5. Serve on individual salad plates. Enjoy!

7 Turkey Kebabs on Bed of Spinach

(serves 4)

Ingredients

1 pound ground turkey

½ medium onion, half finely diced and half thinly sliced

1 clove garlic, minced

2 ounces crumbled feta (about ⅓ cup)

½ cup fresh chopped parsley (or 3 tablespoons dried), divided

½ teaspoon salt

¼ teaspoon ground black pepper

Tomato & Red Onion Salad:

1 cup grape tomatoes, quartered

1 tablespoon olive oil

1 tablespoon red wine vinegar

Salt and ground black pepper, to taste

2 cups baby spinach leaves, packed

Eight bamboo skewers (optional)

Directions

1. Soak skewers (if using) in water for 15 minutes.

2. Preheat oven to 375 degrees.

3. In a medium bowl, combine turkey, diced onion, half of parsley, feta, garlic, salt and pepper.

4. Divide mixture in half and into 4 portions per half. Form each portion around skewer and place on baking sheet (without skewers, create football shaped mounds and place on baking sheet).

5. Bake in oven for 20 minutes, until internal temperature reaches 165°F.

6. Meanwhile, prepare Tomato & Red Onion Salad by combining tomatoes, onions, remaining parsley, olive oil, vinegar. Season with salt and pepper.

7. Divide spinach leaves equally amongst 4 serving plates. If you prefer slightly-cooked spinach (also called wilted spinach), place plate filled with spinach in microwave for 15 seconds.

8. Serve kebabs on spinach and top with tomato salad. Enjoy!

Craving starch? Try serving turkey kebabs on prepared orzo (with or without wilted spinach) and top with tomato salad!

Bonus Recipes

One recipe from the stories of each chapter

CHAPTER 1: ANCHO PORK AND HOMINY STEW

CHAPTER 2: CHOCOLATE LAVA CAKE

CHAPTER 3: TOFU AND CASHEW LETTUCE CUPS

CHAPTER 4: ARUGULA SALAD WITH ROASTED BEETS AND
GOAT CHEESE

CHAPTER 5: LINGUINI WITH CLAMS

CHAPTER 6: PEANUT BUTTER BLUEBERRY
BANANA SMOOTHIE

Ancho Pork and Hominy Stew (serves 4-6)

Ingredients

2 tablespoons ancho chili powder (or regular chili powder)

2 teaspoons dried oregano

1 ½ teaspoons smoked paprika

1 teaspoon ground cumin

½ teaspoon salt

1 ½ pound pork tenderloin, trimmed and cut into ½-inch pieces

2 tablespoons olive oil, divided

1 large onion, diced

1 green bell pepper, diced

1 red bell pepper, diced

1 tablespoon minced garlic

2 ½ cups chicken stock

1 can (28 ounces) hominy, drained

1 can (15 ounces) fire-roasted diced tomatoes

Chopped cilantro, for garnish

Shredded Mexican cheese, as desired

Directions

1. Combine chili powder, oregano, paprika, cumin and salt in a bowl. Set 1 ½ teaspoons aside.

2. Toss pork pieces into spice mix. Coat evenly.

3. Heat 1 tablespoon oil in heavy saucepan or Dutch oven over medium-high heat. Add pork and cook 5 minutes, stirring frequently, until the meat is browned and fragrant.

4. Remove pork from pan.

5. Add remaining olive oil. Add onion, bell pepper and garlic. Sauté 5 minutes until tender.

6. Return pork to pan. Add broth, hominy, tomatoes and reserved spices. Bring to a boil, reduce heat and partially cover to simmer for 25 minutes.

7. Serve with cheese, if desired, and garnish with cilantro. Enjoy!

Recipe adapted from Cooking Light

CHAPTER 2:

Chocolate Lava Cake (serves 4)

Ingredients

4 teaspoons sugar

½ cup butter (1 stick)

4 ounces semisweet chocolate, broken into 1-inch pieces

1 cup confectioners' sugar

2 eggs

2 egg yolks

1 ½ teaspoons instant coffee granules

1 teaspoon vanilla extract

¼ cup plus 2 tablespoons all-purpose flour

½ teaspoon salt

Whipped cream or vanilla ice cream, as topping, if desired

Directions

1. Preheat oven to 400°F.

2. Grease the bottom and sides of four 6-oz. ramekins. Sprinkle each with 1 tea-spoon sugar. Place ramekins on a baking sheet; set aside.

3. In a medium microwave-safe bowl, melt butter and chocolate for 30 sec-onds. Stir, then return for 15-second intervals. Continue stirring at each interval until smooth.

4. Stir in confectioners' sugar until smooth.

5. Whisk in the eggs, egg yolks, instant coffee and vanilla.

6. Stir in flour and salt. Spoon batter into prepared ramekins.

7. Bake 12 minutes (internal temperature should be 160°F), until cake sides are set and middle is soft.

8. Remove ramekins from oven to cool for 5 minutes.

9. Carefully run a small knife around cakes to loosen. Invert warm cakes onto serving plates. Lift ramekins off cakes.

10. Serve warm with whipped cream or ice cream, if desired. Enjoy!

CHAPTER 3:

Tofu and Cashew Lettuce Cups (serves 4-6)

Ingredients

2 tablespoons canola oil

14-ounce package firm tofu, drained and cut into 1-inch squares

2 cloves garlic, minced

1 tablespoon ginger, grated

1 bunch scallions, trimmed and sliced

½ cup shredded carrots

8-ounce can sliced water chestnuts, drained and chopped

⅓ cup roasted, unsalted cashews, chopped

2 cups cooked brown rice

1 small head of Boston or Bibb lettuce, leaves separated

Sauce:

¼ cup soy sauce

¼ cup honey

1 tablespoon Asian chili sauce

Directions

1. Combine sauce ingredients in a small bowl. Set aside.

2. Heat oil in a large skillet over medium-high heat.

3. Cook garlic and ginger until golden and fragrant, 1 minute.

4. Add tofu, stirring occasionally until browning begins, about 3 minutes.

5. Add the scallions and carrots and cook for 1 minute.

6. Stir in water chestnuts and soy sauce mixture. Cook until heated through, about 2-3 minutes (if needed, thicken with 2 teaspoons cornstarch dissolved in 2 tablespoons cool water).

7. Remove from heat and add cashews.

8. Divide the rice among the individual lettuce leaves. Repeat with tofu mixture. Serve immediately. Enjoy!

CHAPTER 4:

Arugula Salad with Roasted Beets and Goat Cheese (serves 6)

Ingredients

6 cups arugula, rinsed and dried

6 fresh beets, washed/scrubbed and ends trimmed*

3 ounces fresh goat cheese, crumbled

¼ cup dried cherries

¼ cup slivered almonds

Dressing:

½ cup white balsamic vinegar

1 medium shallot (thinly sliced)

2 tablespoons honey

⅔ cup extra virgin olive oil

Directions:

1. Preheat oven to 400°F.
2. Whisk together Dressing ingredients, season with salt and pepper, set aside.
3. Wrap beets in a foil packet and roast in oven for 45 minutes. Remove from oven and let cool.
4. When cool enough to hold, peel beets with hands (wear disposable gloves so they don't turn red).
5. Dice beets.
6. Toss arugula, beets and dried cherries in a large serving bowl with just enough dressing to lightly coat. Save extra dressing in fridge.
7. Top with goat cheese and almonds. Serve and enjoy!

*Save time and avoid steps 1-4 by purchasing peeled & pre-roasted beets found in refrigerated produce case at the grocery store.

CHAPTER 5:

Linguini with Clams (serves 2)

Ingredients

  1-2 cans clams (12 fresh clams)

  ¼ cup olive oil

  3 garlic cloves

  ½ teaspoon salt

  ¼ teaspoon ground black pepper

  ¼ cup parsley, chopped

  ½ pound linguine or spaghetti

  ¼ cup grated Romano/Parmesan

Directions

  1. Heat oil in skillet over medium-high heat. Stir in garlic to lightly brown.

  2. Add pepper, salt, parsley and liquid from clams. Simmer 5 minutes.

  3. Add clams. Simmer 1 minute and add cheese.

  4. Pour over linguini. Enjoy!

Thank you, Mom, for giving me this recipe so long ago!

Peanut Butter Blueberry Banana Smoothie (serves 2)

Ingredients

- ½ cup vanilla yogurt
- ½ cup milk
- ¼ cup quick oats
- ½ large banana, fresh or frozen
- ½ cup frozen blueberries
- 2 tablespoons creamy peanut butter

Directions

1. Combine all ingredients in blender.
2. Blend on high for 1 minute until smooth.
3. Pour into two glasses. Enjoy!

Thank you to my daughter Becca for developing this recipe!

REFERENCES

1. U.S. Department of Health and Human Services and U.S. Department of Agriculture. *2015-2020 Dietary Guidelines for Americans*. 8th Edition. December 2015. https://www.dietaryguidelines.gov/sites/default/files/2019-05/2015-2020_Dietary_Guidelines.pdf.

2. U.S. Department of Agriculture. "MyPlate Plan". *ChooseMyPlate*. Updated December 2018. https://www.choosemyplate.gov/myplateplan.

3. Miller, Gregory. "What's Fat Got to do with Type 2 Diabetes?" *National Dairy Council*. https://dairygood.org/content/2016/whats-fat-got-to-do-with-type-2-diabetes.

4. National Institutes of Health. "Vitamin D: Fact Sheet for Consumers". Updated August 2019. https://ods.od.nih.gov/factsheets/VitaminD-Consumer/.

5. Miller, Gregory. "Ask Dr. Dairy: What's the Difference Between Fermented and Probiotic Foods?" *National Dairy Council*. https://dairygood.org/content/2017/ask-dr-dairy-whats-the-difference-between-fermented-and-probiotic-foods.

6. Craig, Winston. "Nutrition Concerns and Health Effects of Vegetarian Diets." *Nutrition in Clinical Practice*. 2010. Volume 25, Issue 6, 613-620.

7. Mayo Clinic Staff. "Vegetarian Diet: How to Get the Best Nutrition". *Healthy Lifestyle: Nutrition and Healthy Eating.* July 2019. https://www.mayoclinic.org/healthy-lifestyle/nutrition-and-healthy-eating/in-depth/vegetarian-diet/art-20046446.

8. Environmental Working Group. "Dirty Dozen". *Shopper's Guide to Pesticides in Produce.* https://www.ewg.org/foodnews/dirty-dozen.php.

9. Willett, Walter C. "Ask the Doctor: Coconut Oil and Health". *Harvard Health Letter*. Published May 2011. Updated August 2018. https://www.health.harvard.edu/staying-healthy/coconut-oil.

10. Cooper, Emily. "Cutting Boards: The Fundamental Tools for Food Prep". *Food & Nutrition*. March 2019. https://foodandnutrition.org/from-the-magazine/cutting-boards-the-fundamental-tools-for-food-prep/.

11. Coyle, Daisy. "Is Nonstick Cookware Like Teflon Safe to Use?" Healthline. July 2017. https://www.healthline.com/nutrition/nonstick-cookware-safety.

12. "Microwaving Food in Plastic: Dangerous or Not?" *Harvard Health Publishing*. Published February 2006. Updated September 2017. https://www.health.harvard.edu/staying-healthy/microwaving-food-in-plastic-dangerous-or-not.

13. U.S. Department of Health & Human Services. "Safe Minimum Cooking Temperatures Charts". FoodSafety.gov. Updated April 2019. https://www.foodsafety.gov/food-safety-charts/safe-minimum-cooking-temperature.

14. Priceconomics. "Here's How Much Money You Save By Cooking At Home". *Forbes*. July 2018. https://www.forbes.com/sites/priceonomics/2018/07/10/heres-how-much-money-do-you-save-by-cooking-at-home/#45504efd35e5.

15. Gunders, Dana. "Wasted: How America is Losing Up to 40 Percent of Its Food from Farm to Fork to Landfill". *Natural Resources Defense Council*, 2017. https://www.nrdc.org/sites/default/files/wasted-2017-report.pdf.

16. FoodPrint. "The Problem of Food Waste". *FoodPrint Issue*. https://foodprint.org/issues/the-problem-of-food-waste/#easy-footnote-bottom-44-1309

17. Vogliano, Chris et al. "The State of America's Wasted Food and Opportunities to Make a Difference". *Journal of the Academy of Nutrition and Dietetics*. Volume 116, Issue 7, 1199-1207.

ABOUT THE AUTHOR

Photo Credit: Kelly Swartz

Lynn Dugan, MS, RDN, translates the science of nutrition to a practical application in the kitchen. She is the founder of MyPlate2Yours, LLC, and helps others make healthy eating a reality by conducting cooking classes, both privately and corporately. She is an Adjunct Faculty Member in Nutrition at Benedictine University and authors a blog on her website, www. myplate2yours.com. Her nutrition tips and culinary skills have been featured on WGN-Chicago, NBC5-Chicago and ABC7-Chicago.

Lynn is currently an active volunteer in her community. She serves on the Glenbard High School District 87 Wellness Committee and teaches nutrition in an after-school program at a local elementary school.

Lynn is a registered and licensed dietitian/nutritionist and holds a master's degree in exercise physiology. She previously worked for a cardiologist conducting clinical research in foods and pharmaceuticals and has published some of this work in the *Journal of the American Medical Association*. Lynn has also authored numerous professional publications. This is her first book for consumers.

Connect with Lynn on social media:

www.myplate2yours.com

Twitter: @myplate2urs

Find myplate2yours on Instagram, Facebook, YouTube and *Pinterest*